This
Prayer Journal
Belongs To:

walk
BY
faith

How to Use This Prayer Journal

Prayer is the most powerful tool that God has given to you. In Jeremiah 29:12, God tells us: "Then you will call on me and come and pray to me, and **I will listen to you.**" Through prayer, you can communicate with God directly!

However, prayer isn't just about sending God requests. It is God's deepest desire that we **seek his presence** and **grow as spiritual beings**. Regardless of the cards that we get dealt in life. God loves you so much that he sent Jesus, his one and only son, to the world. So you shall not perish, but have eternal life (John 3:16).

With this **Prayer Journal**, you can **deepen your relationship with God**.

Here's how to use it:

• **Bible Verse:** Every day, start with reading a few Bible verse. If it's short, copy the verse. Or simply write down the Bible book, chapter and verse (Luke 2:15).

• **What I Can Learn From This:** Close your eyes, be silent. Contemplate what God is trying to teach you through this Bible verse. Write it down.

• **Thank You For:** Gratitude is the key to living a positive life. Often, we are so focused on what goes wrong in our life, that we don't notice all the beautiful things God gives us every day! Write down at least 2 things you are grateful for.

• **I Ask You To:** After you have contemplated the Bible verse and practiced gratitude, you are now in the right mindset to share with God any request you may have. Write them down.

By **keeping a Prayer Journal**, you are building a strong relationship with God. And, by writing everything down, you can keep track of how **your life changes through prayer!**

Date:

Bible Verse

What I Can Learn From This...

Thank You For...

I Ask You To...

Date:

Bible Verse

What I Can Learn From This...

Thank You For...

I Ask You To...

Date:

Bible Verse

What I Can Learn From This...

Thank You For...

I Ask You To...

Date:

Bible Verse

What I Can Learn From This...

Thank You For...

I Ask You To...

Date:

Bible Verse

What I Can Learn From This...

Thank You For...

I Ask You To...

Date:

Bible Verse

What I Can Learn From This...

Thank You For...

I Ask You To...

Date:

Bible Verse

What I Can Learn From This...

Thank You For...

I Ask You To...

Date:

Bible Verse

What I Can Learn From This...

Thank You For...

I Ask You To...

Date:

Bible Verse

What I Can Learn From This...

Thank You For...

I Ask You To...

Date:

Bible Verse

What I Can Learn From This...

Thank You For...

I Ask You To...

Date:

Bible Verse

What I Can Learn From This...

Thank You For...

I Ask You To...

Date:

Bible Verse

What I Can Learn From This...

Thank You For...

I Ask You To...

Date:

Bible Verse

What I Can Learn From This...

Thank You For...

I Ask You To...

Date:

Bible Verse

What I Can Learn From This...

Thank You For...

I Ask You To...

Date:

Bible Verse

What I Can Learn From This...

Thank You For...

I Ask You To...

Date:

Bible Verse

What I Can Learn From This...

Thank You For...

I Ask You To...

Date:

Bible Verse

What I Can Learn From This...

Thank You For...

I Ask You To...

Date:

Bible Verse

What I Can Learn From This...

Thank You For...

I Ask You To...

Date:

Bible Verse

What I Can Learn From This...

Thank You For...

I Ask You To...

Date:

Bible Verse

What I Can Learn From This...

Thank You For...

I Ask You To...

Date:

Bible Verse

What I Can Learn From This...

Thank You For...

I Ask You To...

Date:

Bible Verse

What I Can Learn From This...

Thank You For...

I Ask You To...

Date:

Bible Verse

What I Can Learn From This...

Thank You For...

I Ask You To...

Date:

Bible Verse

What I Can Learn From This...

Thank You For...

I Ask You To...

Date:

Bible Verse

What I Can Learn From This...

Thank You For...

I Ask You To...

Date:

Bible Verse

What I Can Learn From This...

Thank You For...

I Ask You To...

Date:

Bible Verse

What I Can Learn From This...

Thank You For...

I Ask You To...

Date:

Bible Verse

What I Can Learn From This...

Thank You For...

I Ask You To...

Date:

Bible Verse

What I Can Learn From This...

Thank You For...

I Ask You To...

Date:

Bible Verse

What I Can Learn From This...

Thank You For...

I Ask You To...

Date:

Bible Verse

What I Can Learn From This...

Thank You For...

I Ask You To...

Date:

Bible Verse

What I Can Learn From This...

Thank You For...

I Ask You To...

Date:

Bible Verse

What I Can Learn From This...

Thank You For...

I Ask You To...

Date:

Bible Verse

What I Can Learn From This...

Thank You For...

I Ask You To...

Date:

Bible Verse

What I Can Learn From This...

Thank You For...

I Ask You To...

Date:

Bible Verse

What I Can Learn From This...

Thank You For...

I Ask You To...

Date:

Bible Verse

What I Can Learn From This...

Thank You For...

I Ask You To...

Date:

Bible Verse

What I Can Learn From This...

Thank You For...

I Ask You To...

Date:

Bible Verse

What I Can Learn From This...

Thank You For...

I Ask You To...

Date:

Bible Verse

What I Can Learn From This...

Thank You For...

I Ask You To...

Date:

Bible Verse

What I Can Learn From This...

Thank You For...

I Ask You To...

Date:

Bible Verse

What I Can Learn From This...

Thank You For...

I Ask You To...

Date:

Bible Verse

What I Can Learn From This...

Thank You For...

I Ask You To...

Date:

Bible Verse

What I Can Learn From This...

Thank You For...

I Ask You To...

Date:

Bible Verse

What I Can Learn From This...

Thank You For...

I Ask You To...

Date:

Bible Verse

What I Can Learn From This...

Thank You For...

I Ask You To...

Date:

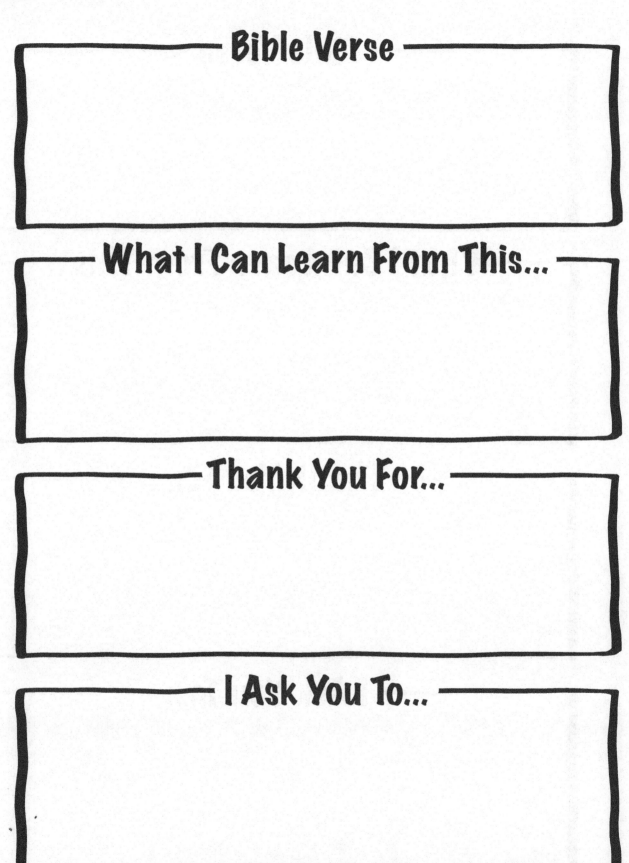

Bible Verse

What I Can Learn From This...

Thank You For...

I Ask You To...

Date:

Bible Verse

What I Can Learn From This...

Thank You For...

I Ask You To...

Date:

Bible Verse

What I Can Learn From This...

Thank You For...

I Ask You To...

Date:

Bible Verse

What I Can Learn From This...

Thank You For...

I Ask You To...

Date:

Bible Verse

What I Can Learn From This...

Thank You For...

I Ask You To...

Date:

Bible Verse

What I Can Learn From This...

Thank You For...

I Ask You To...

Date:

Bible Verse

What I Can Learn From This...

Thank You For...

I Ask You To...

Date:

Bible Verse

What I Can Learn From This...

Thank You For...

I Ask You To...

Date:

Bible Verse

What I Can Learn From This...

Thank You For...

I Ask You To...

Date:

Bible Verse

What I Can Learn From This...

Thank You For...

I Ask You To...

Date:

Bible Verse

What I Can Learn From This...

Thank You For...

I Ask You To...

Date:

Bible Verse

What I Can Learn From This...

Thank You For...

I Ask You To...

Date:

Bible Verse

What I Can Learn From This...

Thank You For...

I Ask You To...

Date:

Bible Verse

What I Can Learn From This...

Thank You For...

I Ask You To...

Date:

Bible Verse

What I Can Learn From This...

Thank You For...

I Ask You To...

Date:

Bible Verse

What I Can Learn From This...

Thank You For...

I Ask You To...

Date:

Bible Verse

What I Can Learn From This...

Thank You For...

I Ask You To...

Date:

Bible Verse

What I Can Learn From This...

Thank You For...

I Ask You To...

Date:

Bible Verse

What I Can Learn From This...

Thank You For...

I Ask You To...

Date:

Bible Verse

What I Can Learn From This...

Thank You For...

I Ask You To...

Date:

Bible Verse

What I Can Learn From This...

Thank You For...

I Ask You To...

Date:

Bible Verse

What I Can Learn From This...

Thank You For...

I Ask You To...

Date:

Bible Verse

What I Can Learn From This...

Thank You For...

I Ask You To...

Date:

Bible Verse

What I Can Learn From This...

Thank You For...

I Ask You To...

Date:

Bible Verse

What I Can Learn From This...

Thank You For...

I Ask You To...

Date:

Bible Verse

What I Can Learn From This...

Thank You For...

I Ask You To...

Date:

Bible Verse

What I Can Learn From This...

Thank You For...

I Ask You To...

Date:

Bible Verse

What I Can Learn From This...

Thank You For...

I Ask You To...

Date:

Bible Verse

What I Can Learn From This...

Thank You For...

I Ask You To...

Date:

Bible Verse

What I Can Learn From This...

Thank You For...

I Ask You To...

Date:

Bible Verse

What I Can Learn From This...

Thank You For...

I Ask You To...

Date:

Bible Verse

What I Can Learn From This...

Thank You For...

I Ask You To...

Date:

Bible Verse

What I Can Learn From This...

Thank You For...

I Ask You To...

Date:

Bible Verse

What I Can Learn From This...

Thank You For...

I Ask You To...

Date:

Bible Verse

What I Can Learn From This...

Thank You For...

I Ask You To...

Date:

Bible Verse

What I Can Learn From This...

Thank You For...

I Ask You To...

Date:

Bible Verse

What I Can Learn From This...

Thank You For...

I Ask You To...

Date:

Bible Verse

What I Can Learn From This...

Thank You For...

I Ask You To...

Date:

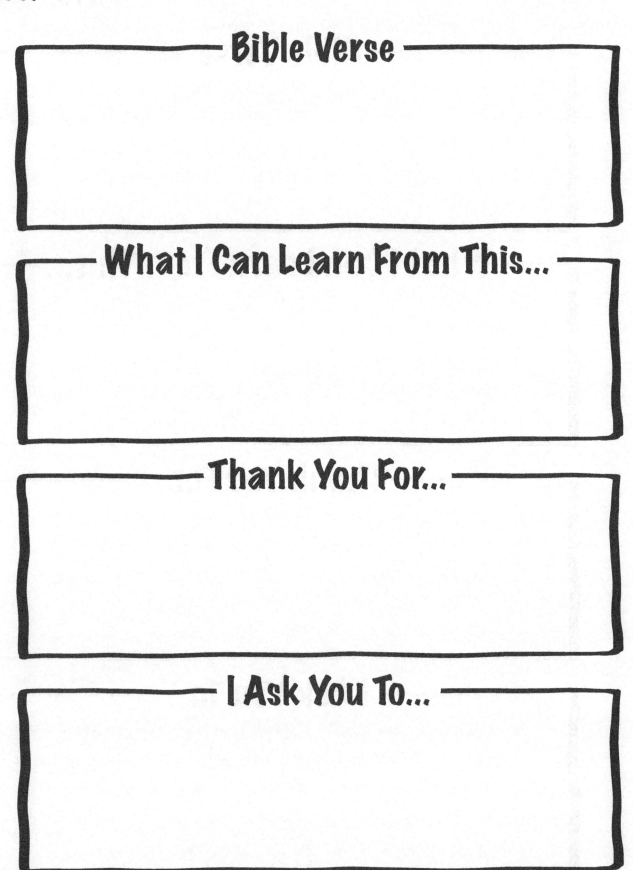

Bible Verse

What I Can Learn From This...

Thank You For...

I Ask You To...

Date:

Bible Verse

What I Can Learn From This...

Thank You For...

I Ask You To...

Date:

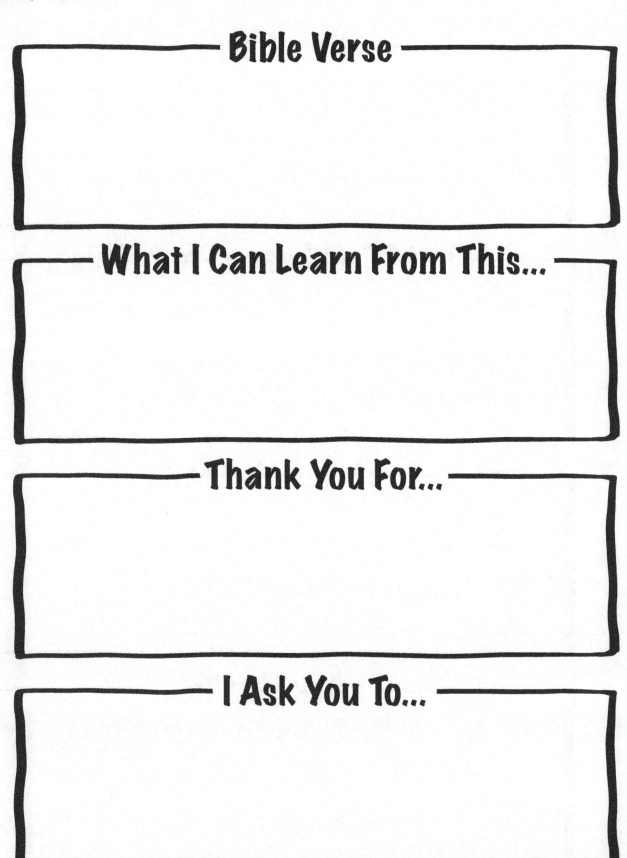

Bible Verse

What I Can Learn From This...

Thank You For...

I Ask You To...

Date:

Bible Verse

What I Can Learn From This...

Thank You For...

I Ask You To...

Date:

Bible Verse

What I Can Learn From This...

Thank You For...

I Ask You To...

Date:

Bible Verse

What I Can Learn From This...

Thank You For...

I Ask You To...

Date:

Bible Verse

What I Can Learn From This...

Thank You For...

I Ask You To...

Date:

Bible Verse

What I Can Learn From This...

Thank You For...

I Ask You To...

Date:

Bible Verse

What I Can Learn From This...

Thank You For...

I Ask You To...

Date:

Bible Verse

What I Can Learn From This...

Thank You For...

I Ask You To...

Date:

Bible Verse

What I Can Learn From This...

Thank You For...

I Ask You To...

Date:

Bible Verse

What I Can Learn From This...

Thank You For...

I Ask You To...

Date:

Bible Verse

What I Can Learn From This...

Thank You For...

I Ask You To...

Date:

Bible Verse

What I Can Learn From This...

Thank You For...

I Ask You To...

Date:

Bible Verse

What I Can Learn From This...

Thank You For...

I Ask You To...

Date:

Bible Verse

What I Can Learn From This...

Thank You For...

I Ask You To...

Notes

Made in the USA
Columbia, SC
19 November 2019